BOGNOR REGIS
THEN & NOW
IN COLOUR

SYLVIA ENDACOTT & SHIRLEY LEWIS

To Lisa Stone and her generation, whose willingness to learn about the past gives us great hope that the future will be in safe hands.

First published in 2012

The History Press
The Mill, Brimscombe Port
Stroud, Gloucestershire, GL5 2QG
www.thehistorypress.co.uk

British Library Cataloguing in Publication Data.
A catalogue record for this book is available from the British Library.

ISBN 978 0 7524 8284 2

Typesetting and origination by The History
Printed in India.
Manufacturing managed by Jellyfish Print Solutions Ltd

CONTENTS

Acknowledgements   4

Also by the Authors   4

Introduction   5

Bognor Regis Then & Now   6

ACKNOWLEDGEMENTS

This book has been made possible by the generosity of many people who have given their time, knowledge and expertise. We have used images from our own collection, however, specific thanks must go to Mick Large for the use of postcards from his collection and to Ron Iden, for the loan of his photographs. We would like to thank past and present members of the Bognor Regis Camera Club, who have joined with us in the taking of the modern images, a task that was not as easy as first envisaged. These include Mandy Colwell, Thelma Cox, Steve Hall, Martin Stone, and Rachel and Roland Waghorn. Special thanks to Steve Hall for his assistance with some of the older images. Thanks also to Cathy Jupp and Marilyn Endacott for their proof reading and comments regarding the contents of this publication. Finally, as ever, to Ron Iden for sharing his historical knowledge and for his welcome comments.

ALSO BY THE AUTHORS

Butlin's: 75 Years of Fun!
Reflections of Bognor Regis

INTRODUCTION

According to modern holiday guides, Bognor Regis is a seaside resort on the coast of West Sussex. However, this is only part of the story. It uniquely has its own birthday, the 18th of January, which is when Sir Richard Hotham laid the foundation stone in 1787 for a 'purpose-built bathing place', thus providing the local historian with a specific date for the start of the modern town's existence.

For many people the town is viewed as a seaside joke, a failed resort, or just a place to retire. Yet many people choose to live and work here in order to enjoy the climate and the town's proximity to the South Downs, the sea and London. Numerous people have arrived here through their work, as we did, and have stayed. At one time, the town was promoted on the London underground as being a most suitable area in which to live and commute to other areas, including London. Another time, it was felt that Bognor Regis was more respectable than Chichester!

We moved to the town as a result of our work, both being employed by Butlin's Holidays at their centre in Bognor Regis. When we finally settled in the town, we subsequently became interested in local history and, in 1979, joined the Bognor Regis Local History Society.

The bygone images in this publication are drawn from our own collection and those of Mick Large, a local postcard collector, and local historian Ron Iden. For the modern images we have engaged past and present members of the Bognor Regis Camera Club, of which Sylvia is also a member. Regarding the selection of pictures, we have shown the changes that would be observed whilst on a walking tour of the town. In respect of the villages, many of which were mentioned in the Domesday Book, these appear at the end of the book purely for ease of reading.

At the time of writing, Bognor Regis is expanding rapidly, with many new estates being constructed due to the urgent needs of an increasing population, and to comply with the Government's housing policy. Different building styles and varying trades have undoubtedly changed the landscape over the years. Large homes have been turned into a series of flats; companies which at one time employed 2,000 people are now being transformed into small work units or shops, and, in some cases, demolished to make way for the out-of-town supermarkets.

As this book is being prepared for publication, we are aware that in the coming months several properties will be changing hands due to the current economic climate. Therefore this book could be an instant history book in the true sense as shops, owners and trades pass into history.

Sylvia Endacott and Shirley Lewis, 2012

HOTHAM PARK HOUSE

WHEN SIR RICHARD Hotham settled in the town from Merton in Surrey in 1787, he decided to build his home within fields and a wooded area. From the front of the house he had an open vista to the sea. On 18 January 1787, the following was recorded in the South Bersted Parish register by the Revd Thomas Durnford: 'The first foundation stone of a Public Bathing Place at Bognor in the Parish of Berstead was laid by Sir Richard Hotham Knt. at the house called by the name of The Lodge.' The foundation stone was for Bognor Lodge (demolished in 1937). Hotham Park House (or Chapel House as it was known originally) was built to the north of Bognor Lodge in the early 1790s. Chapel House, an elaborate building, was built by Sir Richard Hotham as his own residence. Sir Richard went on to build numerous premises in the new resort, which he hoped would rival Brighton. However, this did not occur until after his death in 1799. (Ron Iden collection)

THIS RESIDENCE, BUILT by Sir Richard Hotham, does not appear to have changed outwardly bewteen 1800 and 1947, during which time it was owned by a series of families who made various marks on the town in their own particular way. On the death, in 1941, of the last private owner and town benefactor, William Fletcher, it was requisitioned by the army in the Second World War. After the war, in 1946, it was purchased by the Bognor Regis Urban District Council, who leased the house to the Government Ministries and, in 1947, opened the grounds of this house to the public, naming it Hotham Park. In 1977, the house was saved from demolition and converted into five self-contained apartments. Over the years the town has attracted many royal visitors, culminating in 1929 with the visit of King George V and Queen Mary, when the King convalesced at Craigweil House. Subsequently, the town received the suffix 'Regis'. Opposite the house lay open land until 1959, when it was agreed that Sir Billy Butlin would lease the land from the Council and build one of his last holiday camps. (Photo by Sylvia Endacott)

FIRE STATION, HIGH STREET

THE LEFT-HAND building was originally known as No. 8 High Street when it was purchased in 1899 and plans drawn up for the Fire Brigade's new station by the Town Surveyor, Mr Oswald Bridges. On the ground floor were the appliance bay and stables, while on the first floor was an office and a large room for meetings and recreation. The total cost of the building was £322. Above the first floor windows are the letters B.U.D.C., standing for Bognor Urban District Council. Adjacent to this building we see the shallow bow-fronted Albert Terrace, which was built by the Southerton family and recorded in the 1861 census. The first-floor windows originally had hoods above the balconies, but by the time this photo was taken the balconies had already been removed. The first shop in Albert Terrace was opened in the 1870s by Mr Ezra Royston, selling footwear and general clothing. We can also see the garage of Evershed & Companies' Sussex

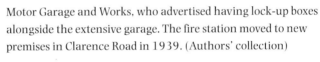

Motor Garage and Works, who advertised having lock-up boxes alongside the extensive garage. The fire station moved to new premises in Clarence Road in 1939. (Authors' collection)

THE ORIGINAL FIRE station building is shown to best effect with the arrival of The Lock Centre Security Company, which moved from the small lock-up shops in front of the railway station when they were demolished. They took over the building in 1996 and have retained the historical façade, including the notation on the top of the building – AD 1899. The first house in Albert Terrace was demolished and a new building constructed, which displays the date 1929, when there was quite an expansion of buildings within the town. This building, now occupied by Chichester College Training Centre, has been Tracey's Furnishings, Bell's Restaurant and even a Chinese restaurant over the years. Only three of the original bow-fronted buildings remain, with modern shops below and flats above. Note that these houses have had their hoods removed and show a clean, uncluttered appearance. The garage shown in the earlier picture has now gone, along with many other small companies where it was possible for the motorist to purchase petrol from the swing-armed pumps over the pavement. (Photo by Martin Stone)

THE WILLIAM HARDWICK, HIGH STREET

THIS HIGH STREET view from the early 1900s shows a number of shops on the left-hand side, including Ernest Richardson, selling decorating materials, who took over No. 7 from the Tate family. Number 9 was occupied by Hawkes the grocers between 1872 and 1970, and No. 11 was occupied by Arthur Cox. On the right-hand side can be seen a public house, constructed by William Hardwicke in 1810 on what was little more than a country lane with views across the meadows to the sea. This coaching inn, originally known as the New Inn, was the departure point for stagecoaches on their nine-hour journey to London and was described as a 'good house of entertainment and well conducted.' It was also used by Bognor's first Council for their meetings. In 1822, the Local Board

of Commissioners was established to run the town affairs and held their meetings here. The inn's first name change – to The Sussex Hotel – came in the 1840s, and in 1987 it was renamed The William Hardwicke, after the original builder. This photo was taken by R. Briant Burgess, Stationer, one of several printers and publishers of postcards, books and pamphlets in the town. (Mick Large collection)

A QUICK GLANCE seems to show no changes, although on closer inspection there have been many. The original three shops on the left have been replaced by modern, brightly coloured façades, while Barclays Bank, with its new frontage, remains on premises it has occupied since 1900. Beyond the pub/hotel on the right-hand side, the trees in private gardens began to disappear from 1914. In that year, a block of shops was built on the corner of London Road and the High Street, and Staley's clothes store took over the shop on the corner, which extended into the High Street. By the mid-1930s they had bought Camden House and Gardens, which was between their store and The William Hardwicke public house, thus removing the last private house in that area of the High Street. Today, Bonmarche operates from this store. The William Hardwicke has now extended to the pavement with its continental-style patio, complete with colourful hanging baskets which brighten up the High Street. The pub enters the annual Bognor in Bloom competition and over the years have won Best Licenced Premises category. The garage which used to be situated beside The William Hardwicke has been transformed into a car park. (Photo by Martin Stone)

ORLANDO TEA ROOMS, HIGH STREET

KNOWN AS No. 13 the High Street when it was first constructed around 1870, this building was part of a terrace of houses situated across the road from The Sussex coaching inn. It was possible to purchase a cup of tea and a sandwich from the front window, and around 1910 it became known as The Orlando Tea Rooms and advertised as the Dining and Refreshment Rooms, which, according to this picture, sold a wide range of alcoholic drinks. Eventually, in 1949, it became known as The Orlando public house. To the left we can see Cucumber Dairy, owned by H. & E. Cox, which offered families 'new milk and cream twice daily from their farm,' as well as the intriguing claim, 'special cows specifically for children and invalids'. To the right was part of Frederick Place, the home of Dr Charles Osborn, who died in 1885 having been Medical Officer of Health for the Bognor Local Board. (Authors' collection)

THE CURRENT VIEW shows Oceans with its modern open-fronted façade. This licenced premise is on the site of the former Orlando Tea Rooms, which has had several name changes over the years, including The Hogs Head and The Beach. Today, it is possible not only to have a pint of lager for £2.60, and buy a full English breakfast for £2.69, but you can also now sit and watch live Sky Sports – a far cry from a cup of tea and a cake from the front window. Between Oceans and the adjacent Worx hairdressers, you can still see the original doorway and steps which led to Dr Charles Osborn's home. The upper floors of both these premises still retain their original features. The dark blue building on the left is part of Clock Walk, with its modern shops and café, which was built in 1985. Prior to this it had been Olby's, Bognor's own department store, with eighteen departments, a coffee lounge and a car park at the rear, which unfortunately closed on 1 September 1984. (Photo by Martin Stone)

YORK INN, HIGH STREET

THE YORK INN is an impressive-looking public house which was built around 1830 and referred to as a Post House in the Pigot's Directory of 1839. It was also described as a wine cellar and was owned by James Smith when it was attached to York House on the corner of the High Street and York Road. The green tiles were a distinctive feature of the Portsmouth Brickwoods Brewery Group. To the left of the inn we can see the original doorway to Barclays Bank. To the right, we can catch a glimpse of the Arcade, which was constructed in 1902. The ornate-covered way, with shops beneath, was constructed by local builder William Tate in the grounds of York House. The Arcade was built at a time when it was a relatively new fashion from France to have covered walkways for shopping. We

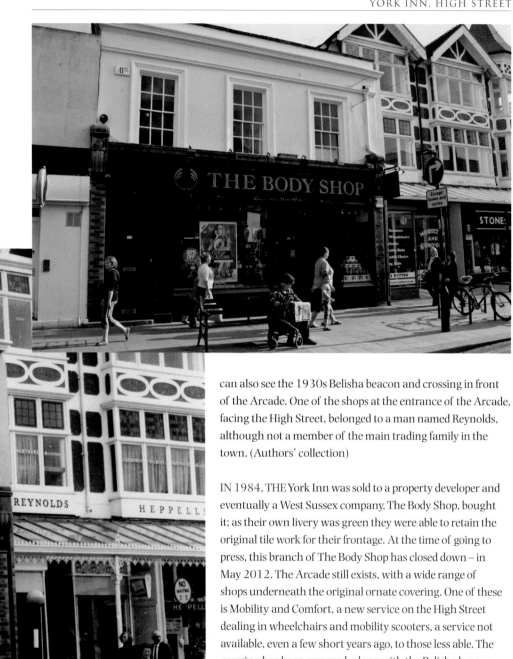

can also see the 1930s Belisha beacon and crossing in front of the Arcade. One of the shops at the entrance of the Arcade, facing the High Street, belonged to a man named Reynolds, although not a member of the main trading family in the town. (Authors' collection)

IN 1984, THE York Inn was sold to a property developer and eventually a West Sussex company, The Body Shop, bought it; as their own livery was green they were able to retain the original tile work for their frontage. At the time of going to press, this branch of The Body Shop has closed down – in May 2012. The Arcade still exists, with a wide range of shops underneath the original ornate covering. One of these is Mobility and Comfort, a new service on the High Street dealing in wheelchairs and mobility scooters, a service not available, even a few short years ago, to those less able. The crossing has been removed, along with the Belisha beacon, and replaced with double yellow lines for parking restrictions and also a blue directional sign, indicating restricted access to a now pedestrianised London Road. Bench seating is now placed at intervals along the street for the benefit of tired shoppers. Bicycle racks are also positioned around the town as an enticement to decrease car use. (Photo by Martin Stone)

TIMOTHY WHITES, HIGH STREET

THIS VIEW OF Bognor's main shopping street from around 1930 shows the imposing Timothy Whites Ltd store, which was built following the purchase of land from the Congregational church in 1929. The long front gardens – seen beyond Timothy Whites – slowly disappeared as the houses ceased to be residential and businesses took over, including solicitors, estate agents and a doctors' surgery. On the left-hand side of the road can be seen the Arcade canopy, which extended over the pavement. This was originally intended to enable ladies to alight from their carriages at the pavement's edge and remain dry. On the far side of York Road is the National Provincial Bank and Long and Strickland dispensing chemist. This was the era of the shop blinds, as seen all along the street. When the sun came out a man appeared with a long pole and pulled the blind out over the pavement. However, after rain beware, as the man appeared again, prodded the blind up, and the water that had collected would cascade over unsuspecting passers-by. (Authors' collection)

OVER THE YEARS the Timothy Whites building has been occupied by banks, Paperchase and, today, a Santander Bank. All signs of private houses and gardens are gone; the buildings have been brought forward to align with Santander. Several large constructions now line the High Street, built at various times, and with two or three shops within each building. The entrance to the Arcade can be seen on the left, minus the canopy over the pavement, although there is still a glass mosaic and a clock in the apex. The overhead lighting has long since gone, in favour of lamp posts. This November view was taken the day the Christmas lights were switched on, and on the right we can see the old-fashioned Gasper organ brought in for the day. At the time of writing, the yellow barriers in the foreground are a common sight around the town as major repairs are being carried out. This pedestrian hub of the town centre has limited vehicle access – a long way from the thoroughfare that was first used by horse-drawn vehicles. (Photo by Sylvia Endacott)

BOGNOR MOTORS, HIGH STREET

IN 1926, MRS Esther Cohen purchased the Wesleyan chapel and Sunday school for £3,500 and leased it to her son, Maurice, to open the Bognor Motor Works. The Wesleyan chapel had stood on the north side of the High Street since 1840. The old photograph was taken in 1958 and you can still see the old chapel and Sunday school buildings, while the garage is now known as Bognor Motors. Bell's Restaurant can be seen on the right and Thomas Fenn's café on the left. During the Second World War, the garage had been used to service and repair aero-engines in conjunction with Portsmouth Aviation Ltd. In 1940, the garage was bought by Ronald Kracke and in 1980, when he retired, his son Ian took over the business. The firm was appointed Vauxhall & Bedford main dealers in 1958, a dealership they held until 1980. By the late 1960s, a large canopy was erected, covering the forecourt right up to the pavement, bringing it up to the new building line and hiding the Wesleyan chapel and Sunday school. It wasn't until 1980,

when the area was being demolished to build new shops, that these two buildings were briefly seen again. (Authors' collection)

AFTER THE DEMOLITION of Bognor Motors, along with some adjacent houses and businesses, the complete site was redeveloped with a long, two-storey brick building, which housed two shops. Today, these are Store Twenty One and Blockbusters, who took over the premises in 1980. These shops were built close to the pavement and actually came in line with buildings erected over the last fifty years. Building line regulations had been relaxed in the 1920s, which allowed anyone developing in the High Street to build on the original long gardens. The first buildings to creep forward with new ideas of architecture were the Southdown bus station in 1934 and Cleeves, the photographic shop, in 1929. On the far side of Store Twenty One (out of sight because it remains on the old building line) is William Hill, the bookmakers. This stands on the corner of Bedford Street and, until 2005, housed two shops which were taken over by Portman Building Society for a period. The shop on the right with the bright red facia is Ladbrooks, which took over the property in 2001. Our High Street can no longer be referred to as 'The Prettiest High Street in the Kingdom', however, a few trees have been planted. (Photo by Shirley Lewis)

19

BUS STATION, HIGH STREET

THIS PHOTO FROM the 1970s shows the western end of the High Street with the iconic art deco Southdown bus station at Nos 66-70. Recognised by its cream and green-tiled façade, it also ran its own enquiry and booking offices. Next door, at nos 62-64, the Co-operative department store was built and opened in 1960, with a full range of departments. One item advertised in 1983 was a 14-inch portable Amstrad TV for £169.95. Eventually, with the arrival of out-of-town superstores, the Co-op trade declined and the shop closed in the late 1980s, to be replaced by Tracey's Furniture store. Next door at No. 60, on the corner of Bedford

Street, Cleeves the photographic and chemist shop opened in 1929. Mr Cleeves was a well-known photographer who produced numerous postcards depicting various views of the town. (Authors' collection)

THIS CONTEMPORARY VIEW shows a moderate amount of change. The bus station closed in June 1981 and was demolished in 1993, having been used as an indoor market in the interim period. Today, in its place, we have the car park entrance to Morrison's supermarket. Next door the Co-op building remains but now houses two shops, including Poppins Café and Restaurant on the ground floor with flats above. Cleeves the chemist and photographer remained on the High Street until 1967, when the National Westminster Bank moved into purpose-built premises at No. 60. New buildings have replaced the garage and other small shops along the left-hand side of the High Street. It is still possible to see the façade of the Catholic church in Clarence Road (in the centre of the picture), and the twin finials of the Arcade are also visible. One wonders who took the original picture, as the modern photographer had to use a ladder atop a van! (Photo by Roland Waghorn)

CONGREGATIONAL
CHURCH, LONDON ROAD

THIS POSTCARD WAS published by R. Briant Burgess, who operated his business opposite the Congregational church at the High Street end of London Road. This was originally a lane, known as Dorset Gardens, with Brunswick Terrace and private homes. Note the high walls and trees which surround the private houses, giving a rural feel. It was eventually renamed London Road and, soon after 1900, the area began to lose its residential character and one by one the tiny gardens became shop forecourts. The Congregational church had its opening service on 7 July 1869, after the newly appointed Revd W.H. Dewitt acquired a field at the corner of High Street and London Road. The church was constructed with the support of the Sussex Home Missionary Society when the

church was said to be 'at low ebb.' This new church could seat 300 people. On the right of the road we can see St John's Church, which was consecrated in 1885 and eventually closed in 1971, its last service being in June. It was demolished in 1972 to make way for more shops in the centre of the town. (Authors' collection)

TODAY, THE PEDESTRIANISED London Road is one of the town's main shopping streets. Gone is the dominant Congregational church, demolished in 1930 to make way for commercial buildings. Santander now stands on the site. One of the particulars of the sale of the church was that no alcohol was to be sold on the consecrated land. London Road has developed from a road of mainly houses interspersed with shops, to a major shopping centre featuring well-known companies. Coffee houses encourage customers to enjoy their outside seating, where they can listen to various buskers or singers raising money for charities. At the time of writing, shops are changing hands more frequently than when the road was first constructed. On the corner of London Road is a controversial sculpture that was unveiled in March 2008. It was inspired by 'an ancient sun mask, the great modern seaside tradition of the International Bognor Birdman Rally, and to reflect the town's famed sunshine record.' (Photo by Rachel Waghorn)

STEAD & SIMPSON, LONDON ROAD

THIS 1960s VIEW shows the mid-section of the busy London Road, with plenty of people, bicycles and cars outside the imposing Hansford store. Stead & Simpson, the well-known shoe shop chain, is in the foreground, their window advertising shoe repairs. Next door is Armsdens; the 1960s Kelly's Street Directory shows that the proprietor, B.J. Lewis, sold stationery, wool and art needlework. This would be Betty Lewis, who went on to run her own wool shop. These two shops have new façades but look above the shop front and you can see the original buildings. Next is the Hansford building, which was constructed in 1931 by Joscelyn Hansford on land he acquired from the Congregational Institute. The shop had an imposing façade considered

by many to be years ahead of its time. On the façade he announced 'Men's Wear Specialist', and was referred to as a 'Gentleman's Tailor and Outfitter'. The word 'sell' was never used by Mr Hansford, as he preferred to 'serve' instead. It was at the back of this store that the town library existed for a period, from 1935 to 1964. (Authors' collection)

IF ONE LOOKS above the shops in the modern photo, some of the original buildings are still recognisable, just new windows have been installed. The Card Factory and Costa Coffee have replaced Stead & Simpson and Armsdens, as their signage shows. The very impressive Hansford building, the newest in this section of the street, was pulled down in 1980 and the present building was erected. It now houses four shops and banks on the ground floor, including the Shoe Zone and Halifax Bank. The upper floors consist of offices. Note the lack of vehicles, as London Road is now paved and pedestrianised. On the left of the picture we can see the travel agents, of which there are a number in the town centre, despite their trade diminishing due to the online ability to book holidays. Further along the road we can just see the newer construction, occupied by Peacocks the clothing retailer. The small independent shops have sadly left, due to the increase in the number of out-of-town shopping experiences. (Photo by Rachel Waghorn)

WATER TOWER BUILDINGS, LONDON ROAD

THIS PHOTO OF the Water Tower Buildings was taken in the early 1880s, shortly after its construction in 1879. Bognor's first waterworks was built in a field that stretched up most of the east side of London Road. Boring for the well started in 1874 and took five years to complete. This brick tower, designed by local architect Arthur Smith, had a reservoir and housed the pumping machine above the well. The new waterworks were supposed to transform the lives of Bognor residents, but unfortunately, due to the close proximity of the sea, saltwater seeped into the piped supplies. Hence it was abandoned five years later. By 1925, the Water Tower was used mainly as offices, the tank, however, was kept topped-up for emergencies. The Water Tower was

the temporary home of Bognor Library from December 1930 to early 1935, when the library moved to Hansfords Hall. In 1936 it was finally demolished. To the left of the Water Tower we can see the Roman Catholic primary school, erected in 1889, which moved in 1927 to Glamis Street and was replaced by Central Buildings. In the distance can be seen St John's Church. (Authors' collection)

THERE IS NOTHING in the modern photo of London Road to give any indication that it was taken from the same position as the older picture. The building seen in the centre, with its white upper storey, stands on the site of the old Water Tower and butts on to the 1927 Central Buildings on the left. On the right-hand side is Boots and the adjacent W.H. Smith's, which were built in 1972 on the site of St John's Church. There are four shops under the white façade; Trends, Goodacre Toys, Dexter's the chemist and Store Twenty One. However, since this picture was taken, Trends has been replaced by Pyramid, selling very nice accessories. This end of London Road is not pedestrianized, as cars come out from the parallel Bedford Street on the right into a one-way system. (Photo by Rachel Waghorn)

THE ALEXANDRA, LONDON ROAD

THERE ARE TIMES when premises seem to transcend time and this is the case for The Alexandra. Originally built as two flint and Bognor rock cottages situated in cornfields, one cottage became known as the Alexandra Tavern, adjacent to a bakery, which was probably built around 1860. This was just prior to a time of expansion for Bognor, as the pending railway station became a reality in 1865. In this picture the Alexandra Tavern is highly visible, with its name emblazoned across the building, and also advertising 'Chichester Fine Ales and Stout'. It was owned at this time by the Turner family, who were well known Bognor brewers. Mr F. Byerley owned the bakery and confectioners next door. The bakery was owned by Thomas Waight in 1883, when he also took over the licence of the Alexandra Tavern. In 1840, the site was referred to as being bounded on the north by the Bognor Garden Field (later the Canada Gardens for the Poor), to the south by a piece of pasture belonging to Mrs Sarah Smith, and on the east by Dorset Gardens. (Mick Large collection)

NOW REFERRED TO as 'The Alex', the pub proudly refers to its origins by stating that it has been a meeting house for gentlefolk since 1864, not a claim which can be made by many licenced premises today. During the First World War, beer was only available on two or three days per week, and to maintain income, the pub sold tea and food until supplies returned. At the time of writing, many licensed premises are suffering from lack of customers in an ever-competitive market. While The Alex continues to trade on its traditional service – drinks and meals – they also host a number of modern activities, including a Beaujolais Nouveau evening, live music evenings, and the raising of money for local charities. One of the features of The Alex is the impressive display of flowers and plants that adorn the front, available to purchase from Fleur de Lis next door. Many public houses today advertise themselves on the internet, through sites such as Drinkaware and modern social network sites including Facebook. (Photo by Roland Waghorn)

POLICE STATION, LONDON ROAD

BOGNOR'S FIRST POLICE station was built on the corner of Station Road and London Road for the Sussex Police in 1867. It was a solid-looking flint and brick building, which could be seen by everyone walking up London Road towards Station Road. This was to remain the police station for Bognor for the next seventy-five years until, in 1938, a new one was opened in front of today's police station in London Road. This second station, which was only operational for thirty-nine years, was demolished in 1977, to be replaced by today's station which was constructed behind, whilst the older building was still operational. The current station cost

£629,000 to build and was officially opened by Her Grace Lavinia, Duchess of Norfolk on 19 January 1978. This new station also contained living accommodation for single officers. To the right of the site of the early police station was Albany House, which was demolished in 1930 to enable the building of the Odeon at the beginning of the cinema boom. (Authors' collection)

THE MODERN VIEW of Clarkes shows a building on the site of the former police station, constructed in 1938. The police station was demolished along with a row of railway cottages and was replaced by shops and flats above, as one building. Clarkes is the latest in a number of estate agents to serve the local area from these premises. To the right we can see the Odeon cinema, which was constructed on the site of the demolished Albany House in 1934 and was opened on Saturday 14 July, by Captain C. Pocock, OBE, RN – the chairman of the Bognor Regis Urban District Council. The freehold for the cinema site was £5,000; the cinema was built at a contract price of £14,000 and the equipment cost £3,346 8s 9d. The name is derived from Oscar Deutsch Entertains Our Nation, a company created in 1928 by Oscar Deutsch. The building that still exists retains the shops beneath the façade, but, like so many picture houses, it is now used as a bingo hall. Today, there is now only one cinema in the town, the Picturedrome. (Photo by Martin Stone)

STATION ROAD

STATION ROAD WAS really just a link road between London Road and Linden Road, but was laid to provide access to the new railway station in 1864. At the beginning of the 1900s it was a rather quiet residential area, with the front of the railway station and The Terminus public house. In 1903, John J. Woolley of Station Road advertised as musical instrument manufacturers and importers, with twenty years' experience in London. Another Station Road business was F. & E. Woods, who transported household items including chalk, manure, coal and coke, in addition to supplying road and path-making materials such as flint, beach gravel and sand. In the 1800s, a Mr C.H. Heming, the second postmaster of a place called Sydenham Mills, in Canada, quickly realised that there was confusion between this area and another Sydenham in Frontenac County. The obvious solution was to change the name, but to what? His father, Edward Heming, had emigrated from Bognor, England, and had the solution; he suggested the name Bognor. Hence

from 1 June 1879, Sydenham Mills became officially known as Bognor. Edward Heming returned to Bognor and lived with his wife at No. 2 Canada Villas, seen here on the left in this 1960s view of Station Road. (Ron Iden collection)

THE MODERN IMAGE shows an area that has not changed considerably and Station Road is still a through road, considered by residents to be part of London Road. Station Road became part of a one-way system in 1966. Whilst the road itself is still clearly recognisable, the businesses trading here have changed significantly and now features several take-away restaurants, employment agencies, and an electrical goods shop. Number 2 Canada Villas is today Davis's fruit shop. An architect expressed the view that Station Road presents many problems because 'one side of the road has a completely different character from the other.' He concluded that, 'it would need a considerable amount of careful thought to bring harmony and continuity to the street.' The left-hand side features original residences changed to shop use, while on the right is a parade of shops built in 1938, when the police station and railway cottages were demolished. Business continued to expand and the need for storage became necessary, thus, in 1911, the Depository in Canada Grove was built. This building had space for auctions and within four years it was necessary for another floor to be added, resulting in the imposing building we see today. (Photo by Steve Hall)

RAILWAY STATION

THE TOWN HAD to wait until 1865 for a railway station, and even then rail travel was not without its problems. There was a hurricane in 1897 followed by a fire in 1899, which caused severe damage to the early wooden structures. Following the fire, a brick-built building was designed and constructed in 1902. The new station sported the bow-fronted restaurant we see today and also a newspaper stand, which has provided passengers with their daily newspapers for over 100 years. The station was fronted at pavement level by a decorative wall, which, being of the same brick, enhanced the building itself. Outwardly, there appears to have been few changes to the original building, however, the number of visitors using the station has dramatically increased. Around 1910-11, the number of Sunday school groups visiting by rail exceeded 2,000, at a time when the population of the town was only 5,000. For many weeks there were reports in the local newspapers asking the rail companies if they could reduce or even stop the number of trains arriving in the town. (Authors' collection)

IN 1931, R.C. Sherriff wrote a novel called *The Fortnight in September*, in which he says, 'the train can go no further than Bognor; if the brakes failed the engine would burst through the buffers and run down the main road into the sea.' He concludes, 'It is a perfect seaside station: the engine comes boldly into the town and stops with its heaving chest square to the coast.' Even in the twenty-first century this description of the railway station remains appropriate. Since the early construction, the wall was removed in 1929 and replaced by a parade of lock-up shops. These were then removed in 1993/4 to produce the open, tree-planted area we have today. Following a threat of demolition in 1989, it was made a Grade II listed building as a 'complete example of the seaside terminus station of the Edwardian period', and even today it is still possible to find LBSCR signs from the original station. The newsagent, which was operated by a Mr Hendry for twenty-one years, was then operated by W.E.H. Smith and today continues to offer an important service. In 1972, the station was named Newhaven Harbour, and, in 1982, it was named Folkestone for its part in various films. (Photo by Sylvia Endacott)

GOODACRES, YORK ROAD

THIS MID-1930s view shows York Road at its junction with the Esplanade. On the left-hand side is a mixture of shops, cafés and restaurants, whilst the right-hand side of the road is taken up with the Theatre Royal (originally the Kursaal) with its entrance to Pierrotland. The impressive shop on the left was Goodacres, occupying No. 30 the Esplanade. This toyshop is remembered with affection by locals, especially those who can name at least one toy purchased there. Goodacres was also a tobacconist and stationers, and sold leather goods too. It operated from the early 1920s until 1972. Opposite, and adjacent to the entrance to Pierrotland, there were small shops which sold sweets, ice cream, newspapers and children's beach items. This area was prone to flooding around 1900, and images are available of a postman rowing a boat so that he could deliver the post. This road was very busy with a variety of shops, including the fondly remembered Bijou luncheon and tea

rooms. The Kursaal building had a skating rink and theatre, both of which were heavily utilised. This building also contained Wade the watchmaker, opticians and jewellers, later becoming Walker's. This building was eventually demolished and The Regis Centre took its place. (Mick Large collection)

IN THIS MODERN photo, we see that Mountbatten Court, the block of flats on the left, has replaced Goodacres toyshop, and the building standing proud of that is the beginning of what is left of York Road. On the far right, a section of the Regis Centre is just visible above a stall canopy. The area was redeveloped in the 1970s and the Regis Centre was opened by the Duke of Norfolk on 10 March 1980. The central section, now known as the Plas St Maur des Fosses, was left as an open space for events and functions for the benefit of visitors and residents. Who can forget the colour and excitement of early clown conventions between 1985 and 1994, with the large marquee in the car park where shows and church services were held. The town parade culminated on the Plas St Maur and, for many hours, 'fun' was the name of the game. The site now hosts a regular twice-weekly market which has built up its own clientele, and, as can be seen in this photograph, has made its own colourful mark on Bognor Regis. (Photo by Sylvia Endacott)

BELMONT STREET

THIS IS THE western end of Belmont Street, which
runs parallel with and between the High Street and the
Promenade and was originally known as New Street. This
is an idyllic-looking little road, with every house identical,
even down to the front wall topped with short railings. This
1903 terrace of thirteen houses, known as Kimbell Terrace,
were part of an intended development to be known as The
Cotswold Estate. The complete estate, which included York
Road and the Esplanade, was to comprise between forty
and fifty houses, but was never completed. The thirteen
houses built had a 17ft frontage and contained two sitting
rooms and a kitchen, scullery and domestic offices. On
the first floor there were five bedrooms and further living
accommodation. These homes could be rented out for £65
according to a 1903 newspaper article which, regretfully,
does not mention whether this was per week, month, quarter
or even per annum. On the left we can see the rear of the High
Street shops. At one time, the staff of William Jones were
able to see the cattle as they were walked up the road to the
slaughterhouse situated opposite their premises. (Mick Large
collection)

IN BOTH PICTURES can be seen William Jones' premises, which opened in 1917 selling and repairing cars. During the 1940s, Jones' garage was one of the last to sell 'one star' petrol suitable for Seagull outboard motors. In 1935, plans were approved to allow Mr Jones to expand into premises in Lennox Street on the site of the old *Bognor Observer* offices, where W. Jones & Sons Ltd still operate today. Following the demolition of this area, these superb homes were replaced by new garages that were available to the residents of Mountbatten Court flats, constructed in the 1980s. This modern view bears no resemblance to the original image due to mass demolition. It is now mainly a road at the rear of the Esplanade flats and High Street shops, where people park their car for an hour whilst shopping in town. Just out of the picture to the far left, next to Reynolds, can be found the original wine/beer store of Buckle and Clidero, the 'High Street Grocers'. They were known as 'Bognor Regis's Leading Provision Store' in 1932. This has recently been renovated and transformed into a converted detached townhouse, at a cost in excess of £225,000. As a nice touch, they have reinstated the original signage on the front of the building. (Photo by Martin Stone)

WATERLOO SQUARE

WATERLOO SQUARE IS one of the older areas of the town, having been a residential area since the early 1800s. Initially laid out as Hothamton Field, it contained a number of fishermen's cottages, and on a 1835 plan it was shown as Waterloo Row on the west side of the Square, with a 'field in the middle', which was to be laid out as a public garden. The garage in the photograph was run by Sait & Gale from 1924 until 1948. Looking at the fashion, the authors date this image to the late 1940s. This garage was originally the site of Bognor's fire station (from 1874 to 1899), and was taken over in 1903 by Norman Wilmott's garage, seen in the photo. Adjacent is a large snack bar owned by W. Kohan from 1953 to 1964, who advertised 'Parties catered for'. The much smaller Tea Box snack bar is next door and adjacent is M.E. Smith, which sold china and fancy goods, in addition to stationery. Behind the tree can be seen part of the Waterloo

Inn, sometimes referred to as being the oldest pub in Bognor Regis. (Mick Large collection)

THE MODERN VIEW shows that there have been many building changes, but some roof lines still remain. The Peri Peri House – offering free deliveries – has replaced M.E. Smith's fancy good's shop. Just out of view, the Waterloo Inn still plies its trade. The central section of shops in the old view, which included the Tea Box and the large snack bar, were replaced in 1990 by Monarch Amusements Cash Casino. The roof line of this new building was designed to fit in with the roof line of the remaining original buildings. This new building overlooks, to its left, a miniature crazy golf course with a good floral display. In front and to the right is the bowling green. The original footpath across the Square, shown on early maps, still exists. In 1929, the Methodist church was constructed within the Square. The area has featured in a number of television programmes including, in 1991, the series *Hope it Rains*, featuring a seaside wax museum. (Photo by Thelma Cox)

THE STEYNE

THE STEYNE WAS developed between 1820 and 1840 on land known as Woodman's Meadow. It was laid out as a central lawned garden with houses facing each other on each side. The lawns and gardens were originally for the sole use of the residents. This became a very fashionable area in the mid-nineteenth century. The most well-known building is No. 9 the Bath House, built around 1824 by James Smith, an early developer in the town and shown in the photograph beyond the gap. The house was let as furnished apartments, where seawater baths could be taken in the basement. The open ground adjacent consisted of a garden with the seawater-pumping machinery. The pair of buildings in the foreground belong to the private Lyncott Hotel, whose restaurant was open to non-residents. The taller building adjacent is Hanover House Hotel. The houses shown beyond Bath House were advertised around 1856 as 'marine retreats for families of distinction'. It is reputed that Noel Coward holidayed here when he was writing *Cavalcade*. It is amusing to see that the cars are parked beside not one, but two 'no parking' signs! (Authors' collection)

THE WHOLE AREA of the Steyne has been subject to a Preservation Order since 1981, and most buildings are listed as being of special interest. The Steyne stands today as a reminder of the town's former Georgian splendour. The Lyncott Hotel has been replaced by the Queen Elizabeth II public house, whose inn sign depicts the famous Cunard liner. Adjacent to this is Richmond House, which replaced the Hanover House Hotel after it was demolished. In 1964, the open area next door was built on and today we have Langford House, comprising of flats, next to the original Bath House, which is also flats. The paved area in the foreground is being well used by the pub for seating and advertising. It would appear that car parking at the seaward end of the Steyne remains an on-going problem. Although this area has been paved over, cars continue to drive over it to reach the Esplanade. In 1983, there were discussions during which it was stated that until the area was landscaped with bollards being erected, the problem would continue. Today, brick-walled gardens, seating and bollards are in place, which has eradicated the problem. (Photo by Shirley Lewis)

CHAPEL STREET

THIS PHOTOGRAPH (RIGHT) shows the cottages at the
northern end of Chapel Street in 1969. Chapel Street was one
of the back streets developed in the 1820s to house the growing
working-class population in the expanding town. It was a
cul-de-sac running north from West Street, mainly made up of
terraces of small cottages with one beer house named The Eagle/
The Globe. These cottages were entered from the pavement and
some older Bognor residents remember seeing people sitting
outside their front doors, chatting or doing chores such as shelling
peas. In 1824, one of the cottages was converted into a Wesleyan
chapel, which remained in use until 1840, when a new chapel
was opened in the High Street. Chapel Street was so-named after
this temporary Wesleyan chapel. It is interesting to look at old
street directories to ascertain who lived in the roads, for example,
in 1916 we find that C. Bishop was a bath chair proprietor and G.
Brooks a bookmaker. Within these forty houses, we can also find
names that are famous within the fishing families of the town, for
example Ide and Masters. (Ron Iden collection)

THE WHOLE OF Chapel Street was demolished in the early 1970s to enable a new health centre to be built. Part of the back of this building, which opened in November 1974, can be seen on the left of the picture. Later, a block of flats (not in the picture) called Seaward Court was built facing onto West Street. Steyne Street was demolished along with Chapel Street, except for a small section at the southern end. This land lay barren until the mid-1980s, when new housing was developed, which can be seen on the right. Arun District Council caused some confusion when they decided to rename the southern remnant of Steyne Street as Chapel Street, to preserve the name. If you look closely at both pictures, you can see in the lower right-hand corner one remaining original feature, a stone-capped brick pillar. There are a number of these stone pillars in this area, and we can surmise that they were gates into the grounds of the large convalescent homes that were demolished to make way for the new Queensway buildings in the 1960s. (Photo by Steve Hall)

WEST STREET

WEST STREET WAS primarily the first shopping centre and is where many of the town's traders commenced business. On the left of the picture are the grounds of the Royal Norfolk Hotel, which opened in 1836. On the right is the Lansdowne Hotel, which is now known as The Ancient Mariner, the front of which is on the Esplanade. It is from this area that the early horse-drawn 'flys' travelled to the railway station at Woodgate to collect passengers to bring into the town. These flys were an early form of taxis. On the right of the street stood The Wheatsheaf public house, from the 1830s until its closure in 1932, when the licence was moved to Hawthorn Road. This street also contains listed buildings such as Portland House, which was built in 1820 and where important visitors were entertained. Further along the street is a blue plaque commemorating the sea artist Joseph Witham. Field's the butchers operated from 1805 in Swansea Lodge, seen on the left of the picture, later moving to premises on the opposite side of the road, and finally closing for good in March 1997. It is now possible to leave West Street via Argyle Road, which was constructed in 1882. (Authors' collection)

WEST STREET IS no longer the major shopping centre it once was. For many years the street was a bustling thoroughfare with its various trades, but today it is more of a drive through to the centre of the town. Some of the street's early traders became very well known – such as Reynolds, which eventually expanded into larger premises in the High Street; however, other trades have declined and their premises turned into flats or homes. The contemporary photograph shows the Bognor Regis Local History Society Museum, which is housed in the premises of the defunct Berkeley Arms. Outwardly, little has changed, although inside the beer barrels and chairs have gone, now replaced by an inviting and very interesting local history museum, providing visitors with an insight into the town's heritage. We can clearly see the boundary of the Royal Norfolk Hotel on the left-hand side, but now it is a complex of housing situated behind the hotel and entered through gates from West Street. (Photo by Thelma Cox)

FIELD HOUSE,
THE ESPLANADE

THE DEVELOPMENT OF this part of the Esplanade began in 1908. Emily Ward, best known
for establishing the Norland Training College, which trained girls to become nannies to the
gentry, came to Bognor in 1880 to convalesce. Around 1900, she started looking into setting
up an establishment for children with their nannies, either for convalescence or holidays.
She first acquired several houses, then Field Row in 1904. In 1908, she began building Field
House, which butted on to Belvoir House on the corner of Gloucester Road and the Esplanade.
In 1911, she added another section with a courtyard in front, acquired Belvoir House and,
in 1926, the final sections of a three-storey block facing Gloucester Road. This explains why
this area always looked such a jumble of buildings. Emily's vision of seaside accommodation
for children and nannies was complete. She had a resident housekeeper and cook and all the

separate parts of Field House had access to a separate kitchen. Emily died in 1930 at the age of 79 following a stroke, but Field House continued until 1939, when the complex was sold. (Authors' collection)

THE HOUSES ON the corner of Gloucester Road and the Esplanade have attracted various comments over the years as the area fell into disrepair. After numerous reports on change of use, finally, in October 1995, demolition took place and the jumble of buildings was removed. In this area today we now have two very distinctive styles of construction. To the left we can see King's Court, built in the late 1970s in a style popular at that time. On the right, covering the corner into Gloucester Road, we have a very different concept. During the building of this modern block, the builders placed digital photographs on the hoardings to give residents an idea of what was to come. When completed, Compass Point was promoted as '24 contemporary apartments overlooking the sea, over five storeys'. The advertising also boasted that each apartment would be able to enjoy the best of Bognor's sunshine, which offers 'plenty for the passer-by to admire.' Compass Point is not popular with everyone, and only history will tell if it stands the test of time. (Photo by Roland Waghorn)

VICTORIAN CONVALESCENT HOME, THE ESPLANADE

THIS CONSTRUCTION ON the seafront was always reported as being a 'fine building', but it was also to become a victim of changing times and in 1980 fell the way of many buildings in the town. Its history began in July 1900, when the Duke and Duchess of York (later to become King George V and Queen Mary) arrived to officially open the convalescent home in memory of Queen Victoria's jubilee. At the same time another home was built alongside called the Princess Mary Memorial Home, named after the Duchess of York's mother, Princess Mary, Duchess of Teck, who died before it was opened. These two eventually amalgamated to become the Victorian Convalescent Home but, possibly due to the length of the name,

was known as Surrey House. Principally, residents were from Surrey, brought to the seaside for 'a rest and a change'. Rising costs and the decline in the need for convalescent homes meant it was eventually to close. (Authors' collection)

BUILT IN 1983, this modern five-storey block of flats replaced the convalescent home, which was demolished in 1980. Named Berkeley Court, it fills the complete site between Clarence Road and Albert Road. This new building still has a small walled area around the property and is complete with an impressive flight of steps to the entrance. In 2012, flats were available for sale in the region of £165,000 for two bedroom and two bathroom apartments with sea views and allocated covered parking – a far cry from the use of the original imposing building. In the 1960s it was thought correct to demolish impressive historical buildings and replace them with modern building styles. The latest construction on the seafront, The Esplanade Grande, has been constructed to imitate an Edwardian era, thus creating dilemmas for future local historians when describing architecture of the past. (Photo by Sylvia Endacott)

COTSWOLD CRESCENT, THE ESPLANADE

ALONG THE SEAFRONT there are varied buildings from a variety of eras. This view from around 1930 shows The Carlton Hotel on the left. Lord William Pitt Lennox laid the foundation stone for Cotswold Crescent on 8 July 1880. It was originally intended to construct a full crescent of thirty-one homes with a proposed 600ft-frontage, however, when it became known that the ground was not stable enough for a construction of the size planned, work ceased, thus just this one section was built. The Duke of Kent, Princess Alexandra and Prince Michael stayed at the Carlton Hotel with their French governess, where their mother, Princess Marina, visited them in the 1940s at weekends. In 1909, approximately thirty years after the

building of Cotswold Crescent, two hotels were built in the Dutch style; namely The Beaulieu and Beaulieu Downs Hotel (seen on the right). In 1965, national newspapers extolled the fact that 'Britain's first teenage hotel' would be soon opening in Bognor Regis. Reg Dwight (later known as Elton John) and others performed at the hotel's club until it was finally closed in 1968. (Mick Large collection)

THE ORIGINAL CARLTON building, minus the interesting chimney stacks, still stands but is today known as The Prom Bar, which is popular all the year round due to its position overlooking the beach and is part of all the summer events. Adjacent is a block of flats which were erected in the 1980s to replace the two original hotels. Named Mountbatten Court, these flats were built in a crescent format, similar to that proposed in the 1880s. In front of the flats the Council has planted a series of grass mounds designed to resemble sand dunes, and while they are not to everyone's taste, over the years they have formed a very pleasant appearance fronting the flats. Originally, this area provided teas and seaside shopping; today a large residence views the activities of the Esplanade, while its occupants enjoy stunning sea views all year round. (Photo by Rachel Waghorn)

BEACH HOTEL,
THE ESPLANADE

THIS POSTCARD VIEW of the Esplanade from around 1914, looking east from the Pier Gates, was produced by Louie Levy, a Frenchman who acquired local photographers' images and transformed them into his own style. We can see horse-drawn carriages situated along the Promenade and family parties enjoying the sea air. The building on the left was originally known as the Beach Inn and was one of the earliest hotels built in Bognor – around 1840. It was in a prime position and overlooked the activities of Mary Wheatland, the town's famous bathing lady with her bathing machines. Next was the Olympian Gardens, a small theatre where it is alleged that Charlie Chaplin failed an audition. Next are several smaller premises before the imposing Carlton Hotel, which was built around 1880. In the distance can be seen Colebrook Terrace, built in 1827, which consisted of four imposing stucco-fronted houses. Over the years they were occupied by Colebrook and

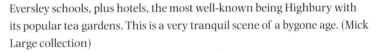

Eversley schools, plus hotels, the most well-known being Highbury with its popular tea gardens. This is a very tranquil scene of a bygone age. (Mick Large collection)

OVER THE INTERVENING years the character of the seafront has changed greatly; the Beach Hotel building still remains; however you will note that it now has a fourth floor, which was added in 1908. Today, the ground floor has a fish and chip take-away and restaurant, which is busy throughout the year. The licence continued until 1963, when the Bognor Regis Urban District Council took over the property. Between the beach and the Carlton, now renamed The Prom Bar, a new casino and four-storey block of flats was constructed in 1992/3, sympathetically to its surroundings, on an area once occupied by a number of smaller premises, including the early Butlin's amusements. This corner was known as Olympian Gardens between 1900 and 1903, before closing in 1930. The fishermen now have a small kiosk on the right of the picture, where they unload their daily catch, although this is much smaller than in the early twentieth century. Note the imaginative lights on each lamp post, which provide the summer Seafront Lights display, running from Gloucester Road to Aldwick. You can even purchase your own light bulb from Bognor Regis Seafront Lights, a voluntary group raising much-needed funds to provide their colourful displays. Cars have now replaced the horse and carriages. (Photo by Rachel Waghorn)

THE PIER

MANY ENGLISH SEASIDE resorts were eager to have a pier and Bognor was lucky to have the nineteenth pier to be built in the UK. The pier was opened on 11 May 1865 and forever changed the way people viewed Bognor's seafront. The pier was over 1,000 feet (305 meters) long and 18 feet (5.4 meters)wide, and took over eighteen months to build at a cost of £5,000. In 1908, after several owners, the pier was sold for just 10s (50p) by the Council and the new owners, Mr Shanley and Mr Carter, spent over £20,000 rebuilding the landward end of the pier. The new attractions and facilities were opened for the 1912 season and included twelve shops and a 1,400-seat theatre, seen in this image. It is interesting to note the small tower on the front of the pier, which was removed, although it is not know when or why. To the right of the pier, on the Promenade, can be seen the office of Mr Jenkins, who operated the bathing machines on this side of the pier. In the foreground are the gardens of Waterloo Square. (Authors' collection)

IN THIS CONTEMPORARY view, the lower pier head is smaller following the removal of the theatre fly tower. It is also noticeable that the pier is much shorter, due to a number of heavy storms from 1965 to the present day, which have demolished various sections. The pier played its part in both world wars; during the First World War it was used by the army and during the Second World War it was renamed HMS *St Barbara* and used as a shore base for the Royal Navy. During the Second World War, a section of the main walkway was removed as part of a national initiative to prevent the enemy using piers on which to land. While the pier's cinema and theatres have gone into decline, it is still very busy and popular, with two nightclubs and amusement arcades attracting today's youngsters. It is also used annually for the Birdman Rally competition, where amateurs endeavour to fly off the end of the pier. In the foreground we can see a lamp post illumination in the shape of a crown, installed in 2002 to celebrate the Queen's Golden Jubilee.

(Photo by Sylvia Endacott)

THE ROYAL HOTEL,
THE ESPLANADE

THIS 1960s VIEW of the seafront is very interesting as it shows a scene long since disappeared, a stretch of the lower Prom. Here we see railings at pavement level and then two drops before reaching the sandy beach. Plenty of people are taking advantage of the beach and sea air. The Royal Hotel is on the far right and is the most imposing building on this part of the seafront. The earliest section of the hotel was originally the Manor House, constructed around 1822 by Richard Dally, the clerk to Bognor's first Board of Local Commissioners – the Council. After a period it was leased to Mr Arthur Binstead, a librarian, who transferred his library stock to this new building, as the encroaching sea in his previous dwelling was creating serious problems for his books. The Manor House then became known as Binstead's Library. The current hotel was built in 1888 and was designed by Arthur Smith, a gentleman who was involved in numerous other major constructions around the town. It was a

very impressive building on the seafront and the 1901 town guide stated that, 'a visitor could imagine themselves to be comfortably ensconced on a yacht' whilst sitting on the hotel balcony. The original hotel was known as the Royal Pier Hotel, and was named thus in the 1903 *Guide to Bognor*. However, after numerous objections, it was renamed and by 1912 became known as The Royal Hotel. (Authors' collection)

THE MODERN PICTURE shows the level of shingle that has covered the beach, necessitating the construction of a new sea wall, which was formally opened July 1991. In 1962, the Royal Hotel was in the news as *The Punch and Judy Man*, starring Tony Hancock, was being filmed on the beach opposite. The film's cast, including John le Mesiurer and Hugh Lloyd, enjoyed their stay at the Royal Hotel. As with many films, notices were placed in the local press for people to come forward as extras, and over 2,000 answered the call. The manager of the hotel, Len Humphreys, and his son Chris, appeared in a scene filmed outside the Town Hall with Ronald Fraser. In 1989, the Royal Hotel became known as an 'International Apartment Hotel', and it was possible to purchase an apartment on a 125-year lease. The first release of these apartments attracted quite a rush of people wanting to purchase a studio apartment for £79,000, plus other charges for leasehold fees and service charges. Today, ten of these apartments are still owned under this 125-year lease. The modern picture shows that the beach level has risen up to meet the newly constructed sea wall, designed to protect the seafront properties from the high tides which occasionally flooded the Esplanade. (Photo by Roland Waghorn)

THE CONNAUGHT HOTEL, THE ESPLANADE

AN ELEGANT EDWARDIAN scene from around 1912, this area of Bognor seafront stretching from West Street to the Steyne was referred to as Victoria Place in the mid-nineteenth century. When first built, there was one long drive in front of all three houses, running parallel to the Esplanade, entered by a gate in front of the Connaught Hotel (on the right of the picture). At some point, all of these houses were turned into hotels. An advertisement in the 1899 Bognor Guide for the Lansdowne Boarding House (the middle building) offered 'home comforts and cleanliness ensured by personal superintendence with good cycling accommodation.' It continued: 'The house faces the sea and commands a splendid view.' The Connaught Hotel was run by Mrs Bertrum Cole and her sons during the 1940s and '50s. It was claimed that their hotel was nearer the sea than any other in Bognor Regis. The final building in this group was, in 1953, the Palatine Private Hotel, and between 1956 and the mid-1970s it was known as the Alanroy Hotel. A nurse can been seen in the middle of this view pushing her charge along the seafront. (Authors' collection)

AS THE ROAD became busier with traffic, the drive was taken away and today you step straight from the buildings onto the pavement and Esplanade. The first building, as seen today, was restructured in 1963. The Connaught Hotel was bought in 1963 by Solar Hotels Ltd. The managing director realised that Bognor Regis had sufficient hotels for visitors, but a shortage of flats, a general impression around the 1960s. Hence he developed the old hotel into twenty-eight self-contained flatlets, each with its own modern kitchenette; each ground floor flatlet had its own paved outdoor space. The conversion also included a launderette with drying and ironing facilities. It was anticipated that these flats would chiefly be occupied by elderly people and let at an affordable rate. There were no great changes to the exterior of the building, except for the addition of two new bay windows on the ground floor. The middle building has flats above, with a ground-level entry to Nos 1 and 2 Little London. The remaining ground floor currently comprises Tuptim Siam, a Thai restaurant. The restaurant and adjacent ground-floor flat were redeveloped as a result of frequent flooding by the sea. (Photo by Shirley Lewis)

ESPLANADE
THEATRE

THIS AREA WAS originally part of the land owned by the Royal
Norfolk Hotel, but was sold to the Council in 1901 for the sum of
£60. A bandstand was erected for use by military bands. By 1913, the
venue was so popular that it was enlarged, with deckchairs around it,
which helped raise £500 for the hire of the bands. Further expansion
took place and on 19 June 1937, at a cost of £3,666, the new band
enclosure was opened with 3,000 people attending the event. By 1945,
more expansion took place and the area was covered and renamed
the Esplanade Concert Hall. By 1951, it was renamed the Esplanade
Theatre and had 720 tip-up seats installed. This venue was very
popular with entertainers, including Tony Hancock, Roy Castle, Dusty
Springfield, Bill Pertwee and Petula Clark, among others. 'Dazzle' was a
very popular summer presentation. In 1968, the summer programme
advised that adults were to be charged 6s, and 1s for children.
(Authors' collection)

SADLY, DUE TO declining audiences and a change in entertainment preferences, it was decided to close the Esplanade Theatre. This happened on 10 February 1980, much to the sadness of the townspeople, and the building was demolished by April 1980. It was the fourth theatre to close in Bognor Regis since the Second World War. There were numerous plans for the future, including a German-style beer garden. A Macari's Coffee Bar operated within the theatre but its lease did not expire until 1987, so the land had to remain bare for seven years. In 1981, students and teachers from Felpham Comprehensive School painted murals on a remaining wall depicting scenes of the town. There was interest shown in having a model boat concession on the site and the suggestion of flats, but ultimately it was transformed into a skateboard park for young people, and today the area is also served by a kiosk selling a range of snacks. The original main walkway to the theatre has been retained and gardens and palm trees have been planted to enhance this area. In the background it is possible to see the modern block of flats known as the Rock Gardens. (Photo by Mandy Colwell)

ROCK GARDENS,
THE ESPLANADE

THE ORIGINAL BUILDINGS, built around 1804, were in a crescent-shaped terrace overlooking their own gardens and out to sea. Built by Daniel Wonham, they consisted of a number of separate houses with some apartments costing 2 guineas per week, until Goodwood fortnight, when the rate increased to 8 guineas. An early trade card of 1814 advertised this crescent of eleven houses: 'Ladies and Gentlemen are solicited to apply to Mr D. Wonham,' continuing, 'who may want a residence at this delightful marine retreat.' The famous librettist, W.S. Gilbert, occupied No. 11 Rock Buildings towards the end of the First World War, where it is alleged he composed 'The Pirates of Penzance'. Later, the crescent consisted of the Rock Gardens, Old Coastguards and Mermaid Hotels, used extensively during the summer months. One gentleman, Reginald George Pullinger, who was born at the Rock Gardens Hotel in 1894, later became head gardener at the hotel. It is

believed that this area was one of the first constructions of 'principal lodging houses', as stated in an 1856 guidebook. (Authors' collection)

DUE TO THE decline in use of the hotels in this crescent, the premises were adapted as bedsits and, by 1965, the local press reported that this area was to be cleared for a block of flats. Interestingly, the area was apparently derelict for more than ten years before it was taken over by the Council, cleared, and the site then offered for flats to be constructed. The west end section was demolished in 1972 and the remainder ten years later. In March 1985, work commenced on the new construction of flats, known as Rock Gardens, comprising sixty-seven privately owned flats. While the flats were erected on the same site, they were given gardens in front to improve the appearance of this stark style of construction, so prevalent during this period. Each generation has a building style that is either appreciated by residents or viewed as being out of keeping with the era. We have here two distinctive styles; the reader has to decide on their own view. There are a variety of flats within this complex and, at the time of writing, a one-bedroom flat costs £179,950. (Photo by Mandy Colwell)

MARINE PARADE,
THE ESPLANADE

THESE SPACIOUS SEAFRONT period houses make up Marine Parade and were built between about 1815 and 1891. This 1920s postcard shows Nos 1-5 from right to left. Number 1 is a Victorian house originally built around 1840, with a further storey added in 1891 by Arthur Smith, featuring a French chateau style roofline. Number 2 – 'Sea House' – is a pretty Regency house tucked into this parade with a striped first-floor canopy. The first house in this parade is shown standing alone on a map of 1817. Numbers 3 to 5 were again Victorian, being completed between 1850 and 1891 with their bow fronts and canopies. Each house had its own small garden in front of it; a private road divided these gardens from a large, private communal grass

area which ran down to the sea. When the public promenade was extended westwards, part of the lawn had to be given up. However, this was in exchange for the construction and maintenance of a flint wall with two pillared gateways, which were built at either end with cast-iron arches overhead. From 1905 to 1934 the occupant of No. 3 was geologist Edmund Martin Venables, who discovered a rich source of fossils on the Aldwick foreshore. (Authors' collection)

THIS PARADE OF houses still has the ambience of a bygone age. Little has changed in this scene; the lawn, wall and gateways are still original, but the cast-iron overhead arches have been removed. The complete terrace was listed for architectural interest in 1973 and the owners of these properties certainly have kept them in excellent order. In the year 2000, No. 1, the Victorian house, was converted into three flats, a common occurrence with so many owners of larger houses being unable to meet the soaring costs of maintaining them. Numbers 3 to 5, which were originally private residences, later became a hotel. In Kelly's directories of 1953 and 1964, these premises were listed as The Marine Parade Hotel with Mrs Jellinck as the proprietor. By 1972, Kelly's directory is listing Nos 4 and 5 as being converted into three flats each. (Photo by Mandy Colwell)

THE MARINE PARK CAFÉ, ALDWICK

THIS LATE 1950s view (right) shows the Marine Park Café standing prominently on the corner of Nyewood Lane and Goodman Drive. Across the road are Marine Park Gardens, and in front the beach provides excellent sea views. The café has had a few changes of status over the years. A 1959 town guide advertisement calls it Marine Park Café and Restaurant, serving morning coffee, luncheons and teas, with a special dining room for parties. In 1963, it is named as Marine Park Café and the Grosvenor Restaurant. Gray's Brothers rented out beach huts in this area, providing a good source of customers. To the left of the café can just be seen a confectionery shop selling toys, films and other beach-related items, which was run by Mr S.F. Stephens for over twelve years. To the right of the café are two private hotels – the Sands Hotel, which was run by the Britton family, and the Alancourt Hotel. In a 1955 guide, the Alancourt Hotel advertised 'the position of this hotel, coupled with its protected balcony, provides an unsurpassed haven for those contemplating winter residence . . .' (Authors' collection)

THE SAME VIEW today has changed considerably. The Marine Park Café has extended further along Nyewood Lane and two storeys of flats have been constructed above. Young's Brewery has a public house and restaurant named The Waverley, still serving morning coffee and afternoon teas in addition to offering a full restaurant service. The outside seating area has been extended with a full roof and a partially enclosed frontage. This caters for those wishing to overlook the sea as well as conforming with new laws which do not allow smoking within the premises. Within the pub itself are numerous large pictures depicting scenes of bygone Bognor. On the left of this photograph a hedge borders Marine Park Gardens, within which can be seen the street sign for Marine Drive West. This road was renamed Marine Drive West in October 1953, as Goodman Drive, as it was known from 1901, gave no indication of the road's proximity to the sea. On the far side of The Waverley, up to Park Road, hotels continue to offer all-year-round accommodation. (Photo by Mandy Colwell)

THE PYRENEES HOTEL, ALDWICK

IN 1926, THE Council bought 23½ acres of land from William Fletcher, a Bognor benefactor and landowner, and the complete area was developed into Marine Park Estate. A brochure published in 1931 by H.W. Seymour, a local developer and builder, advertised houses for sale. The Pyrenees Hotel stood on the corner of Nyewood Lane and Kings Parade in west Bognor Regis. The 1934 Bognor Regis Official Guide stated that 'it stood 100yds from and overlooking the sea, Marine Park Gardens and the putting green.' It went on to say that 'the hotel had 25 bedrooms, all with hot and cold running water and electric or gas fires', all important features for enticing visitors. A late dinner was served at 'separate tables', several garages were available, and a garden for the convenience of guests. This postcard image was taken when the Pyrenees was still functioning

as a hotel. In the 1950s it was promoting itself as having forty bedrooms and 'separate tables', which seemed to be a theme of many hotels. As with many hotels of the time, they also used vegetables from their own garden. However, by 1966 it was empty and awaiting demolition, when the whole area was being developed to house fifty-six flats at a cost of a quarter of a million pounds. (Authors' collection)

THIS BLOCK OF flats was built in 1966/67 on the site of the Pyrenees Hotel. This is confirmed by the position of the postbox still on the corner. However, the young trees planted along Nyewood Lane have now all disappeared. In total, fifty-six flats were built in three blocks around a central courtyard, containing garages and parking spaces for each flat. The flats were originally for sale from £6,250 on a ninety-nine-year lease. Ground rents were from £30 a year, with garages extra. A 1967 brochure stated that 'approach to the flats will be through a side view central courtyard, making it continental in concept with crisp lawns and gay flower borders.' The brochure continued: 'the site is some 50 yards from the beach and twice that distance from the charming little shopping parade of West Bognor Regis, which features service with a smile rather than the Town Centre self-service.' (Photo by Mandy Colwell)

WOOD STREET, ALDWICK

THESE COTTAGES WERE shown on the first edition 1876 Ordnance Survey map. The first two shops appeared in Aldwick Road from the 1870s, when plans were drawn up for the Victoria Park Estate. This also saw the arrival of the post office, still in existence today. It was not until 1896 that more shops started to appear in this area. There was great excitement in 1910 when fifty-eight freehold plots were auctioned and purchased by Dr Alonso Henry Stocker, of Craigweil House, in 1912, with the Aldwick Road parade of shops on land belonging to Mr Edwin Thorp. In the past there had been a wooded area in the vicinity behind Aldwick Road and, when the area was developed, one road was named Wood Street as a reminder of its origins. For many years, Nos 2, 4, 6 and 8 were one unit under the ownership of the Metropolitan Gospel Mission. Both gates are entitled Cottage Homes, whilst plaques on the wall above named them Ebenezer Cottages. (Mick Large collection)

WOOD STREET IS one of those small side roads which has changed very little in almost a hundred years. In October 1948, some of the Mission cottages were for auction by Messrs Tregear & Sons as four freehold cottages. The sale particulars stated: 'The properties standing well back from the road are brick built with cement rendered elevations and slated roofs. They have been well maintained with the benefit of connections to main services of water, gas, electricity and drainage' – facilities we take for granted in the twenty-first century. The arrival of the motorcar seems to have had the biggest impact, with garden walls being removed for car parking and double yellow lines edging all the roads. Now these houses are privately owned, all indications of their past have been eradicated. Today's large-wheeled refuse bins create an untidy look as they cannot be kept out of sight – the terraces having no rear access. In 1987, No. 4 came up for sale at a quoted price of £44,950. Today's house prices are in the region of £175,000. It is interesting to view old street directories as these small cottages once had names such as Woburn, Lennox, Selsey and Portland. These cottages were eventually just plainly numbered – such a shame losing their impressive names. (Photo by Mandy Colwell)

WILMOTT'S GARAGE, ALDWICK

THE NAME NORMAN James Wilmott was well known in the town, with his first premises being the Pier Motor Cycle works in the old fire station on Waterloo Square, which he acquired in 1903. A year later, he was one of the first people to bring the motorcar to the town, when, in 1904, he began dealing in Rover cars. Due to an expanding business, Norman bought land in Aldwick Road just prior to 1914, but was unable to proceed until after the war; consequently his new garage didn't open until 1921. This new garage (seen in the picture) was constructed from an aircraft hangar, previously at the Norman Thompson Seaplane factory in Middleton-on-Sea. During the Second World War, Wilmott's was the only 'pool petrol' garage in Bognor Regis and dealt with the repair and maintenance of RAF and National Fire Service vehicles in the area. The garage was

kept busy with this and running a taxi service for RAF officers to and from Tangmere Aerodrome. This business continued under the name of West End Garage and was run by the family until it was sold in 1976 to the Dove Group of companies. The following year the Dove Group purchased the Pennicotts departmental store next door and was able to extend their services by installing modern equipment in readiness for the new MOT test, which was introduced in 1979. (Authors' collection)

THE SLATED BARN Garage in Aldwick changed hands in 1995. The new owners reinstated attended petrol pumps and went on to acquire a Kia car franchise in 1997. In 2002, the same group bought Wilmott's garage in Aldwick Road from the Dove Group and renamed it Newbarn Garage. The building is still easily recognisable, despite the modern white façade now covering the high arched windows and a generally smarter appearance. Petrol sales ceased at Newbarn in 1999, releasing valuable display space for the Kia car franchise and giving the forecourt a less cluttered appearance. Car prices have increased considerably over the years and are a far cry from the receipt issued by Wilmott's in August 1930, which confirmed that a 10hp Swift 'Foursome' coupe cost £276 15s, which included aluminium numbers for 12s 6d and a licence for the remainder of the year costing £4 7s 6d. Newbarn Garage and Bognor Motors are two long-standing garages in the town still providing their original services. (Photo by Mandy Colwell)

THE SHIP INN, ALDWICK

THE SHIP INN is thought to be over 200 years old but the earliest reference to it is as an alehouse on the 1841 census. Its first publican, Mary Cobden, remained for only one year. Originally, it stood in a country lane surrounded by fields, as seen in this peaceful scene of a bygone age. The horse appears to be the main means of transport, as seen by the only advertisement on the building which states, 'Good stabling'. In the late 1880s, an advertisement described the establishment as 'a Hostelry with good accommodation for families for a shilling per night, with stabling and lock up coach house.' Besides selling alcohol, the inn doubled as a grocer and tea dealer, and, with no shops locally, wood and coal could be ordered. In 1899, when the brewers Henty & Son took over, they installed one Edwin Millar as the innkeeper, whose family remained with the establishment for a further twenty-five years. They also made improvements to the building at this time, using half of the adjoining stable to enlarge the downstairs room and

adding a further bedroom above. It was not until 1930 that a hanging inn sign actually showed a galleon in full sail. (Authors' collection)

SINCE THE 1920s, Aldwick had grown in popularity as a residential area and now the Ship Inn stands in the heart of Aldwick parish on one of its busiest roads. Modernisation of the Ship Inn took place in the 1930s and included the installation of the bay windows. The internal accommodation at this time consisted of a saloon bar and a public bar, plus a bottle and jug area in a passageway – an early type of take-away service. Over the years, The Ship has had many landlords but, in 1970, when the Morrisons arrived as landlords, the Ship Inn became a very popular and widely known meeting place. More changes were made to the accommodation and more upgrading was carried out at this time. The saloon bar was enlarged, the public bar became the restaurant, and the bottle and jug area disappeared. The walls were decorated with paintings and photographs of local scenes, and many old farming implements and horse brasses dating back to the early days of the original Ship Inn were displayed. During the year 2000, the licensee attempted to obtain Listed Building status, as the premises allegedly dates back to 1750; however, they were unsuccessful with their application. (Photo by Roland Waghorn)

THE BEAR, PAGHAM

THIS SMALL COTTAGE alehouse was built around 1840 in
Pagham. It was owned by the Turner family, whose brewery,
established in 1809, was in Mead Lane, off the present Upper
Bognor Road. This brewery remained the main supplier of ale to
local pubs for several decades. The first publican of The Bear was
Robert Cobden, who remained the licensee for ten years. When
built, The Bear stood in a country lane with a few other cottages
around. It was possibly a smugglers' haunt because of its location.
In the early 1900s, Pagham and Nyetimber still consisted of
mainly agricultural land so the majority of the male population
worked on one or other of the several farms in the area. However,
The Bear had competition as in 1860 two licenced premises
opened up, The Lion (formerly The Red Lion) and The Lamb, which
are both still licenced premises today. The original Bear Inn (shown
in the postcard) was actually demolished in 1930 to make way
for today's public house. The Bear is one of the public houses in
Pagham where the annual Boxing Day Pagham Pram Race stops.
It averages fifty entries and over 2,500 spectators have watched
participants complete the three-mile course over the last sixty
years. (Authors' collection)

THE FAMOUS LOCAL artist Ralph Ellis was commissioned in 1924 to paint an inn sign for The Bear, which depicted a bear in chains, indicating that possibly bear baiting occurred at some time in the history of the pub or locality. The modern public house does not have the conventional hanging sign. Their 'logo' now shows a bear, but not in chains. This present-day Bear Inn was built in 1930 on the site of the old public house, and has a style of façade typical of pub premises built around this period. Today's proprietors advertise on the internet with their own website and promote that they have five bedrooms, all with modern facilities, in addition to an extensive menu and light snacks. Promotion of this type of establishment in the twenty-first century is by reference to the past, and The Bear is no exception, which advertises itself as a 'very friendly and welcoming eighteenth-century Free House and bed & breakfast'. Reference is also made to the building being 'full of curiosities' – a visit will have to answer that. (Photo by Steve Hall)

BUTLIN'S

UNTIL THE LATE 1950s, the area between this main
road from Felpham to Bognor Regis was an open area of
land partly taken up by car parks and a model railway,
but things changed considerably when Billy Butlin
built his holiday camp. He had already been operating
amusements and a zoo on Bognor Regis seafront since
1932, but in 1958 the Bognor Regis Council decided
that they wished Billy to move further east along the
seafront. Finally, on 2 June 1960, the centre opened
and was poised to hold 5,200 guests and approximately
1,000 staff. During the first season, they received over
30,000 visitors, who paid in the region of £15 per week
for full board. The building in this picture was the main
reception, dormitories for staff and, in later days, it
housed the Head Office. It was here that Shirley Lewis
worked for a number of years until her retirement in
1996. It was also here, in 1969, that Sylvia Endacott
joined Butlin's as Assistant Personnel Manager. Like
so many other employees, when they left the company,
they stayed in the area and made it their home.
(Authors' collection)

THIS MODERN IMAGE shows very little of the modern holiday centre, mainly because of all the trees which have grown up around the boundary fence. We can also see that the Head Office building has been removed. This image does not show the many new initiatives that Bourne Leisure have introduced since taking over in 2000, because of their location elsewhere on the centre. In August 2005, their Shoreline Hotel was opened, overlooking the sea and named after a hotel once situated on Bognor Regis seafront. Then, in 2010, a second hotel, The Ocean, was opened in the vicinity of the boating lake and outdoor swimming pool (seen on the left of the picture). By the time this book is published their third hotel, The Wave, will be open. It will include 215 bedrooms and twenty-nine apartments over eight storeys, many of which will have sea views. This new hotel will have an Amazon Kindle library, underwater-themed gaming room and iPod docking stations, catering for the twenty-first-century guest. (Photo by Steve Hall)

SNOOKS CORNER, FELPHAM

SNOOKS CORNER IS on the junction of Canning Road and Sea Road in Felpham. The terrace of houses on the far right is the beginning of Sea Road, while the houses on the left are seen beyond their long gardens in Canning Road. A greengrocers shop was set up outside Victoria Cottage in Sea Road by Henry Reynolds in 1884, when his milling business failed. The shop was taken over by Henry Snook in 1916. There was another general shop in the area on the corner of Outram Road from 1898. It is in this area that there existed two windmills, which would have dominated the skyline. We should also remember William Blake, who, in 1803, resided in the village. We have to remember of course that Felpham has a much longer and more detailed history than Bognor, since it was mentioned in the Domesday Book. Many articles and postcard messages refer to outings to Bognor across the fields, as it was quite a separate village for much of its history. (Mick Large collection)

THE SITE OF H. Snook has now been taken over by a garden and the adjacent home has been brightly painted, which is quite appropriate as this area is now home to numerous artists. The horse and carriages have been replaced by the modern cars, while double yellow lines restrict parking in this extremely busy cul-de-sac that leads down to the sea. This area is still referred to as Snooks Corner and there is a community group looking after the interest of this area. It is well worth a visit to walk the three short roads to view these cottages, terraces and houses, which are mainly painted white, cream or pastel shades. Leading off Sea Road, they terminate at the Promenade, with its new imposing sea wall, constructed to help alleviate flooding in this area. Off the picture on the right-hand side is the boundary fence of Butlin's, which leads to the entrance of Longbrook, a grassy area which now contains a number of pieces of keep fit equipment for everyone to use. (Photo by Steve Hall)

RAILWAY CARRIAGES, FELPHAM

HOLIDAY ACCOMMODATION HAS taken all forms over the years, from tents to hotels, holiday centres and bed & breakfast establishments. In 1917, the Homeland Handbooks referred to railway carriages at Felpham and also mentioned that owners could keep a dinghy beneath as the area was liable to flood. Following the First World War, there was a surplus of railway carriages and it was possible for people to purchase them. Some of the railway carriages were erected from 1919 by a Mr A. Jenkins, and also a local company, namely Seymour's, towed the carriages into position. Some were purchased at this time for £500. Archibald Spencer

purchased one in 1920 and named it Merry Moments, to reflect the mood of his visits to the area. To the right of this picture we can see Sea Road. This corner of Felpham has always been popular with visitors to the area. (Authors' collection)

OVER THE YEARS, holiday trends have changed and it is for this reason that, in 1969, the Council planned to remove the railway carriages due to the decline in their use. For many years this space bounded the area known as Longbrook, with an open space behind. Today, this site has Butlin's as a backdrop, where visitors congregate in much larger communities than in the small railway carriages of the 1920s. Sea Road is very vibrant today and annually has an Art Celebration event, where many of the local artists open their homes to promote their crafts. The modern visitor can hire a beach hut in Felpham, as opposed to a railway carriage. One of the carriages similar to those in this picture was for sale for £165,000 at the time this photo was taken, and included three bedrooms, two receptions and one bathroom. (Photo by Steve Hall)

POST OFFICE, ELMER

ELMER ALSO INCLUDES the hamlet of Ancton, centered around Ancton Farm, which is considerably older than Elmer, which has only been developed within the last fifty years. Between 1910 and 1918, this area was famous for being the home of the Norman Thompson Flight Company Ltd. Most of Elmer used to be farmland until the housing drive of the post-war years, when the Elmer Sands Estate was constructed. Much of the original housing in this estate consisted of old railway carriages; over the years these are being replaced by modern housing. Many people are not aware of the location of Elmer, however, for many years this has been a preferred destination for many visitors. Many people first arrived in the area as holidaymakers,

before becoming residents; at one time nearly 10 per cent of the area was holiday homes. Its postal address is 'Elmer, Middleton-on-Sea'. In the shopping area are the local shop, launderette, Indian restaurant and an estate agents, along with two pubs – The Cabin and The Elmer. (Mick Large collection)

THIS MODERN VIEW shows how little has changed, with the Elmer Inn and the Elmer Beach Stores and Post Office still in existence. Traffic to the aircraft works has long since ceased and been replaced by holidaymakers going to the New City holiday centre, which opened in 1923 and was renamed the Southdean-on-Sea Hotel in 1934, all later replaced by housing to cater for the increase in homes for week-enders and visitors wanting to live permanently in this hidden seaside gem. However, within days of this picture being taken, the shop and post office closed due to the arrival of a small Tesco store in the locality. It has since reopened. There are now more residents and an increase in retirement homes in the area. It is a very popular holiday location as well as a much sought after residential area, lying as it does in a quiet area between Bognor Regis and Littlehampton. (Photo by Steve Hall)

ROYAL PARADE, NORTH BERSTED

THIS EARLY 1960s view of the Royal Parade shows the shops of the Newtown Estate. They can be seen at North Bersted on the left as you travel to Chichester on the A259 from Bognor Regis. The foreground is Chichester Road and bearing left is Central Avenue, one of the roads which form the Newtown Estate, along with Bedford Avenue, Southway, Central Drive, Newtown Avenue and Greencourt Drive. G.A. Neal & Sons built this estate between 1932 and 1938, and some of the houses can be seen beyond these shops on Central Drive. The Newtown Estate was prestigious at the time: they built just ten houses to one acre and each house had a road to the rear of their back gardens to enable tradesmen to reach the back of the house without having

to use the front gate. On the corner can be seen Sidcots café, which had originally been the Estate Office. The other shops were a mixture of those found in any parade of shops, including the grocer, butcher, bakers and newsagents. (Authors' collection)

IN TODAY'S SCENE the café has been replaced by the Royal Fish Bar. When the café sign was removed, the original wording – 'Royal Parade 1932' – was revealed. Although a percentage of the homes have undergone structural changes, many can still be found little changed from eighty years ago. During the Second World War, some of the newly constructed homes were used by service personnel associated with the Bognor Regis ALG (Advanced Landing Ground). The trees along Central Avenue have now grown and obscure the houses, however, the two streetlights in the foreground remain. Rarely is there a vacant shop in this parade and today we have a cake shop, pharmacy, Chinese take-away, Indian and Polish supermarket, and a newsagent. When researching local history, it's easy to miss a location and Royal Parade could be such, until you find that the 1960s street directory recorded these shops as being within Central Drive and included a chemist, grocer, cycle and wine stores – not much different from today. Both photographs show a number of parked cars, which would suggest that this parade is as popular now as it was then. (Photo by Martin Stone)

SHEEPWASH LANE, BERSTED

IN ANY TOWN there are numerous roads which form
a spine to a developed area, but of which little is known
to today's driver; here we have such a road. Early maps
show a small lane called Sheepwash Lane, which
contained a sheep dip, some of the land belonging to a
Harry Collyer of South Bersted. By 1904, a later map
shows the road as Cemetery Road. Even as late as 1924
there were still discussions about the name for this
road: a newspaper report argued for it to be changed
to Hawthorn Road – less vulgar, apparently. This view
shows the road from Essex Road towards Chichester
Road. While originally consisting mostly of houses,
there were also a number of trades and businesses in the
road, including a Servite Convent, the Bognor Isolation
Hospital, the Boys' Home for Waifs and Strays, and Mrs
Verion's Laundry. (Mick Large collection)

TODAY, THE SHOP in the foreground of the earlier
picture has reverted to a private residence, but the rest
of the terrace appears to have remained untouched.
The road is now covered, with the familiar orange

to denote a slow-down junction. Further along Hawthorn Road, not shown, other changes have taken place. With the arrival of a new century – 1900 – Bognor Football Club became a feature of the town with its new home in Nyewood Lane, bordering Hawthorn Road. This was considered a retrograde step, as the local press said it would 'take a lot of interest to entice people to go to such an out-of-the-way place.' Today, we tend to think of the road as just a thoroughfare containing homes, but historically it has been home to a great mixture of premises, including schools, garages and shops. Do you remember Olby's? They had numerous shops around the town; their main shop in the High Street closed in 1987, however, their Hawthorn Road shop continued trading until it too closed and was demolished to make way for a Co-op supermarket. In 2007, the Co-op was demolished to allow flats to be built, with a smaller Co-op shop beneath. (Photo by Steve Hall)

POST OFFICE,
SOUTH BERSTED

NUMBER 62 GORDON Avenue. This area was actually laid out in the late 1890s, with freehold being available (according to the local press) in 1902. This shop was recorded as a post office in 1910, and remained as a post office until it was closed in 2008. For a time the postmaster was a Mr G. Burgess. The advertisement for the premises stated that they had a 'dispatch of letters' six times per day between 8 a.m. and 8 p.m., the last collection being at 7.50 p.m. We should remember that for many years it was possible to post mail in the morning and have it delivered the same day. This is an interesting picture and one wonders why the lady is leaning out of the window and what the man is handing to the boy with the bicycle. This image was taken before 1921, as it shows neither the parish hall in Gordon Avenue nor the lock-up shops in Highfield Road, which were constructed in 1921. (Mick Large collection)

AT FIRST GLANCE you could say the building looks as it did in the 1920s. However, take a closer look and we find several alterations: chimneypots removed and the wooden balustrading at roof level replaced with a metal one. The original windows have been replaced with double-glazing and on the right the entrance is now a bay window. A ramp has been installed around the front to enable disabled people access to the shop. In today's economic climate, modern shop owners have to advertise their wares to a much greater extent. The building is now a Premier newsagent, general store and off-licence. Outside we see advertising for lottery tickets and large window posters to attract the public with special offers. Four lock-up shops have been built on the open space to the left of Highfield Road. Number 96 was originally a fishmonger until the mid-1960s, when it became a fish & chip shop. Graham Press, the printers, was here in the early 1970s, but the premises have now been incorporated into the Highfield Fish Bar. As a sign of the times, No. 92 was originally a butchers and is now Bits and Pieces, selling computer items. Number 90, originally shoe repairers and then a fruit shop, is now a launderette. (Photo by Martin Stone)

ESSEX ROAD, BERSTED

AS WE COME to the end of our comparison of bygone and modern Bognor Regis, we take a look at quite an interesting road. Situated parallel to Chichester Road, and linking Town Cross Avenue and Hawthorn Road, Essex Road received planning approval as far back as 17 September 1886 and was built by local builder, Henry Geall. It is recorded on the 1891 town census and on early town maps it is located in an area known as 'New Town' – which, ultimately, was never developed. The road contains quite distinctive houses, of similar design, which have not been altered over the years, except for the inclusion of new windows and doors. Shown in the picture is a shop that has had many uses over the years and, more recently, was a well-known TV and aerial shop until the premises closed in 2011, the owner continuing the business from another

site. In the 1916 directory this road is indicated as leading from Cemetery Lane (Hawthorn Road) to Green Lane (Town Cross Avenue), causing a problem for research if you are unaware of the area's development and history. (Mick Large collection)

ESSEX ROAD, LIKE so many in the town, was constructed in an era of limited personal transportation, so that car parking and garages for small homes was not a consideration of the developers. Fortunately, many of the new estates currently being constructed do have some limited provision for cars. Much of the new housing around the town is linked to famous people or the location, thus we wonder why Essex Road is so-named – perhaps Essex was the original home of the builder? Recently, one new estate was named Hotham Park for a short period, until it was renamed Willows Edge. Had someone not done their homework? We hope you have enjoyed your stroll around Bognor Regis and hope this book will encourage you to stop, look and see if you can detect the changes which have taken place, and, of course, continue to do so. (Photo by Steve Hall)

If you enjoyed this book, then you may also like . . .

Butlin's: 75 Years of Fun!
SYLVIA ENDACOTT & SHIRLEY LEWIS

This nostalgic selection of images illustrates the history of the various camps
and hotels, including all of the things we associate with this most British of
establishments. From Redcoats to water worlds, and from the Glamorous
Grandmothers competitions to National Talent contests, this book provides an
enjoyable and nostalgic trip down memory lane for all who know and love Butlin's,
allowing us a glimpse into the social history of this quintessential British holiday.

978 0 7524 5863 2

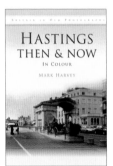

Hastings Then & Now
MARK HARVEY

Hastings and St Leonards have undergone many changes since the Victorian era:
rapid expansion, the impact of two world wars and new developments, including
the erection of housing areas, shops and roads, which have changed the face of
the area forever. In this stunning collection of views, both old and new, postcard
collector and local historian Mark Harvey invites you to take a fascinating and
nostalgic tour of Hastings.

978 0 7524 6208 0

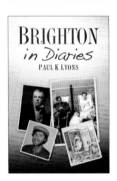

Brighton in Diaries
PAUL K. LYONS

This collection of extracts contains many legendary writers – including Walter
Scott, Arnold Bennett and Virginia Woolf – inhabit these pages, as well as some
less well-known characters, such as William Tayler (a footman), Gideon Mantell
(a surgeon and dinosaur bone collector), and Xue Fucheng (an early Chinese
diplomat). By turn insightful, hilarious and profound, *Brighton in Diaries* will
delight residents and visitors alike.

978 0 7524 6222 6

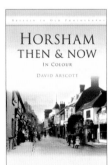

Horsham Then & Now
DAVID ARSCOTT

Few Sussex town centres have changed as dramatically as Horsham, and many
of its residents would be hard-pressed to recognise the location of photographs
taken as recently as thirty years ago. In this book, David Arscott walks the modern
townscape to discover what remains of Horsham's past, and what has replaced
features that have gone for ever.

978 0 7524 6346 9

Visit our website and discover thousands of other History Press books.

www.thehistorypress.co.uk